FISH HUNT

DEDICATION

This book is dedicated to my lovely wife Jenny who has been very patient with me and for her wonderful support.

FISH HUNT

This is a story about inseparable brother cats Mr. Nimble and Meowfinn. They've grown up together and are very close despite having different mindsets and favors. Each brothers' day starts of inventing a new way to get themselves a breakfast. Meowfinn's tricky ideas and Mr.Nimble's inexhaustible energy turn each day into unforgettable adventure that brings joy and new friends.

Glutton and lazybone

Avoids any activity unless it is a food quest

Is ready for heroic deeds for sweets sake

Fortunate and easy-going fellow

With brother's support always succeeds in reaching desired

Active and dexter

Always in a playful mode

Is more into sports rather than video games

Adores brother and supports him in reaching any of his crazy goals

Able to get his lazybone brother outdoors by any means

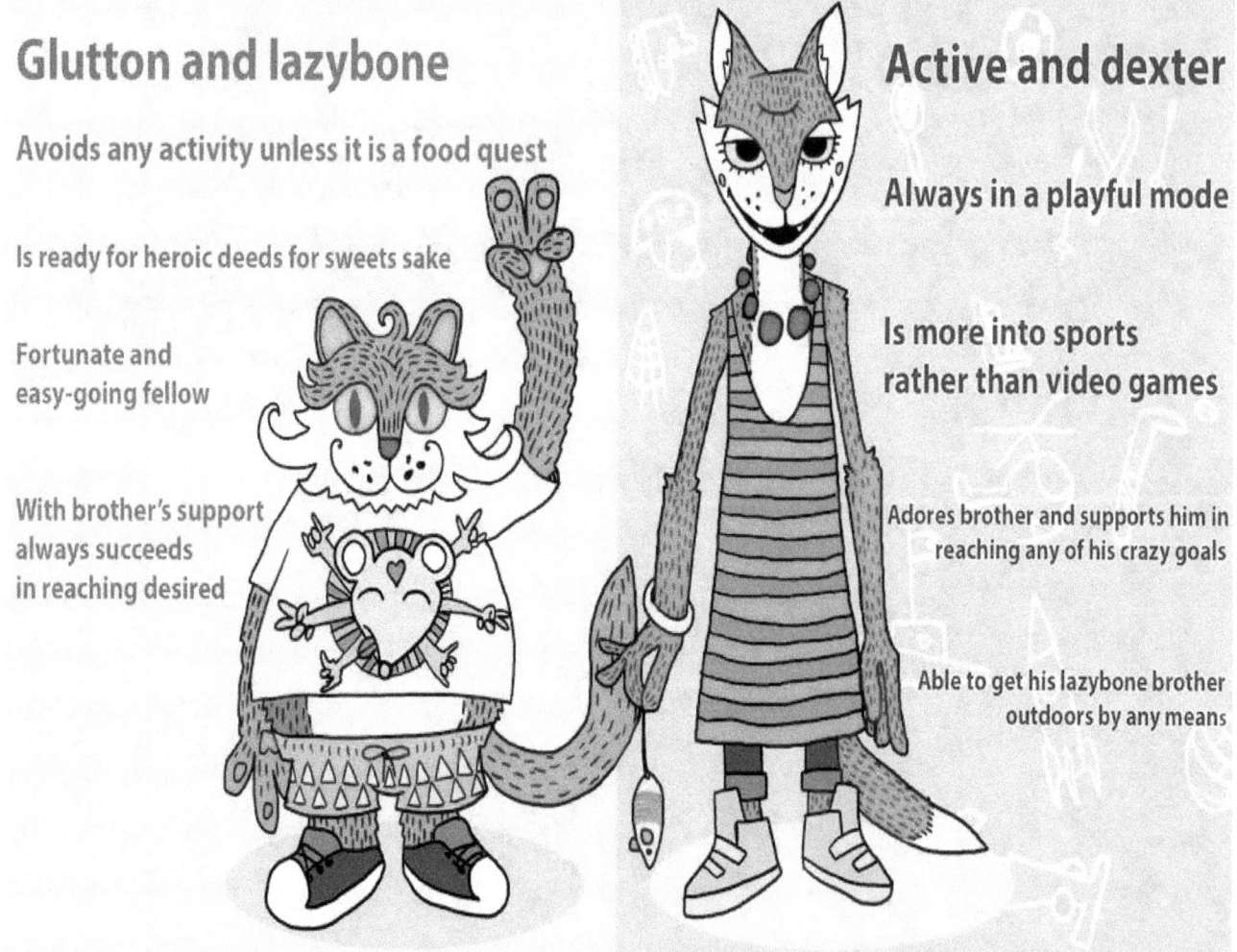

MEOWFINN & Mr. NIMBLE

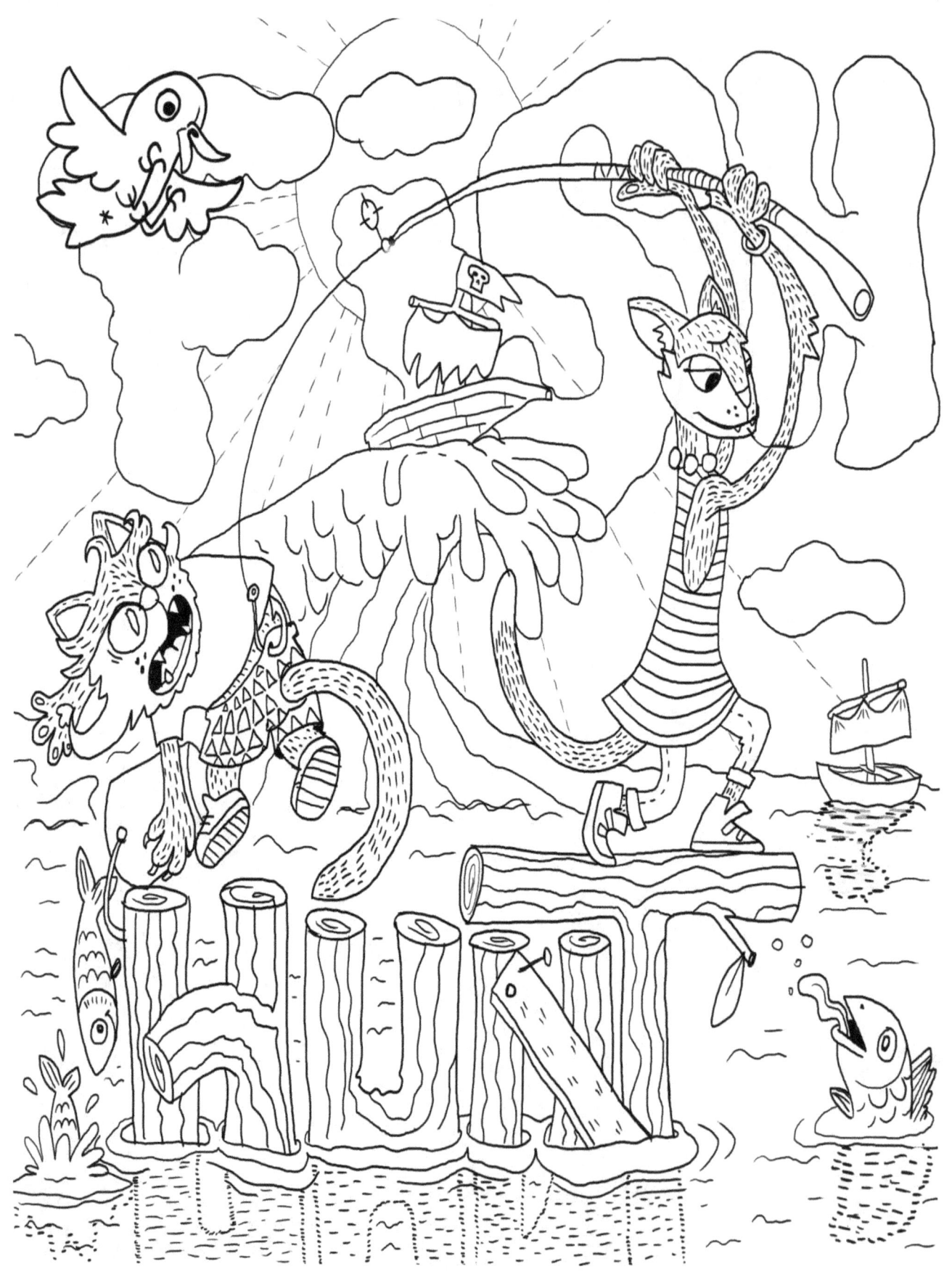

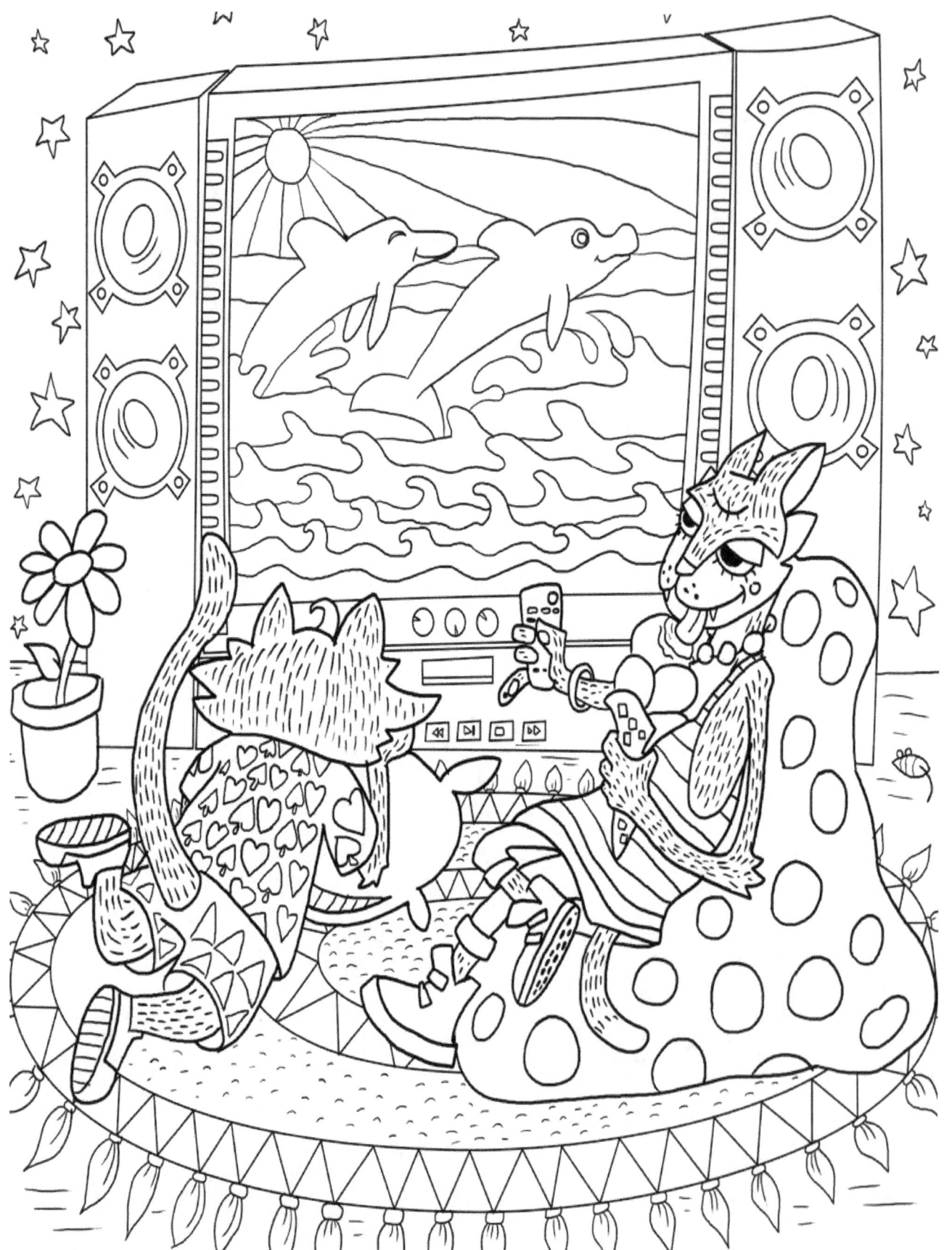

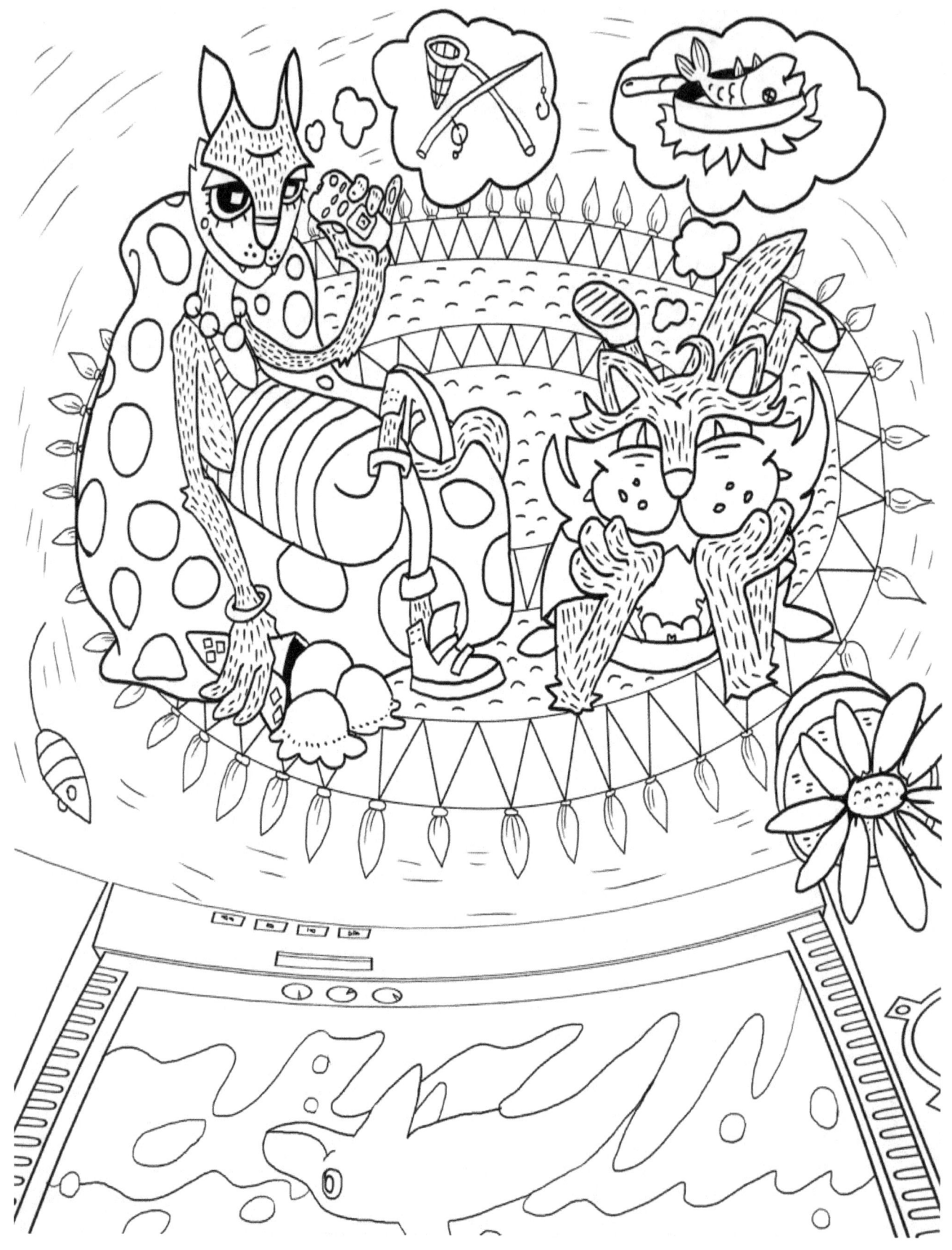

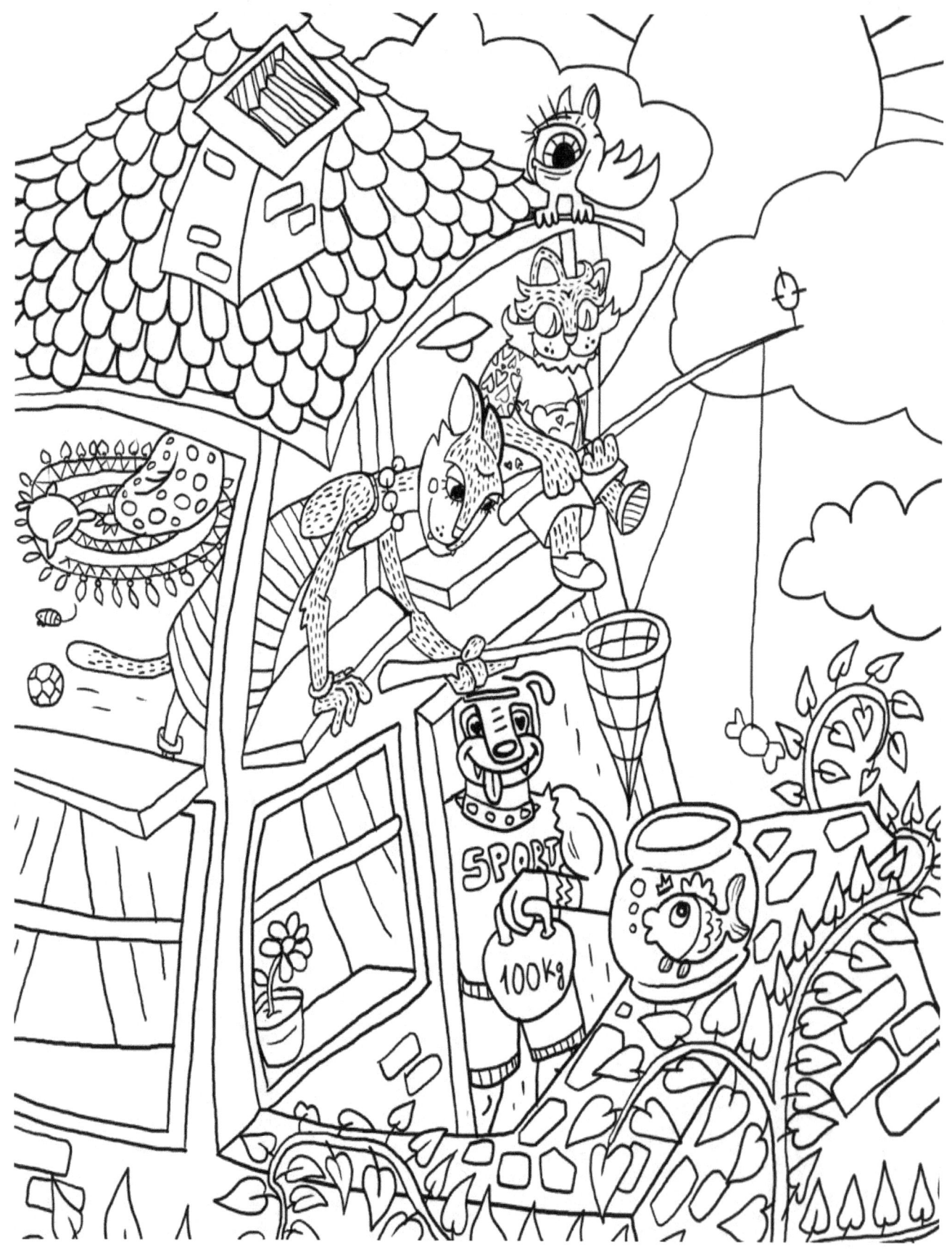

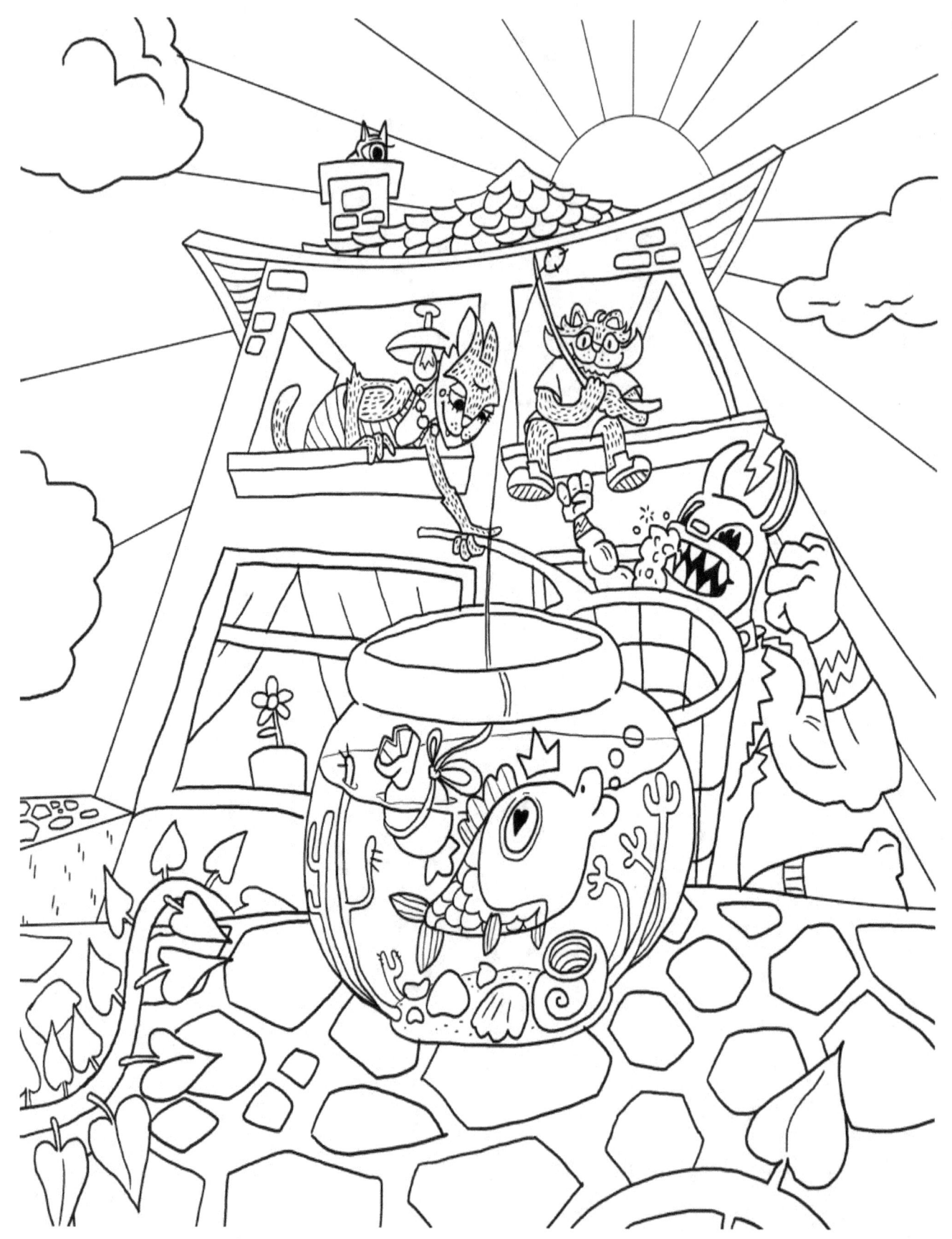

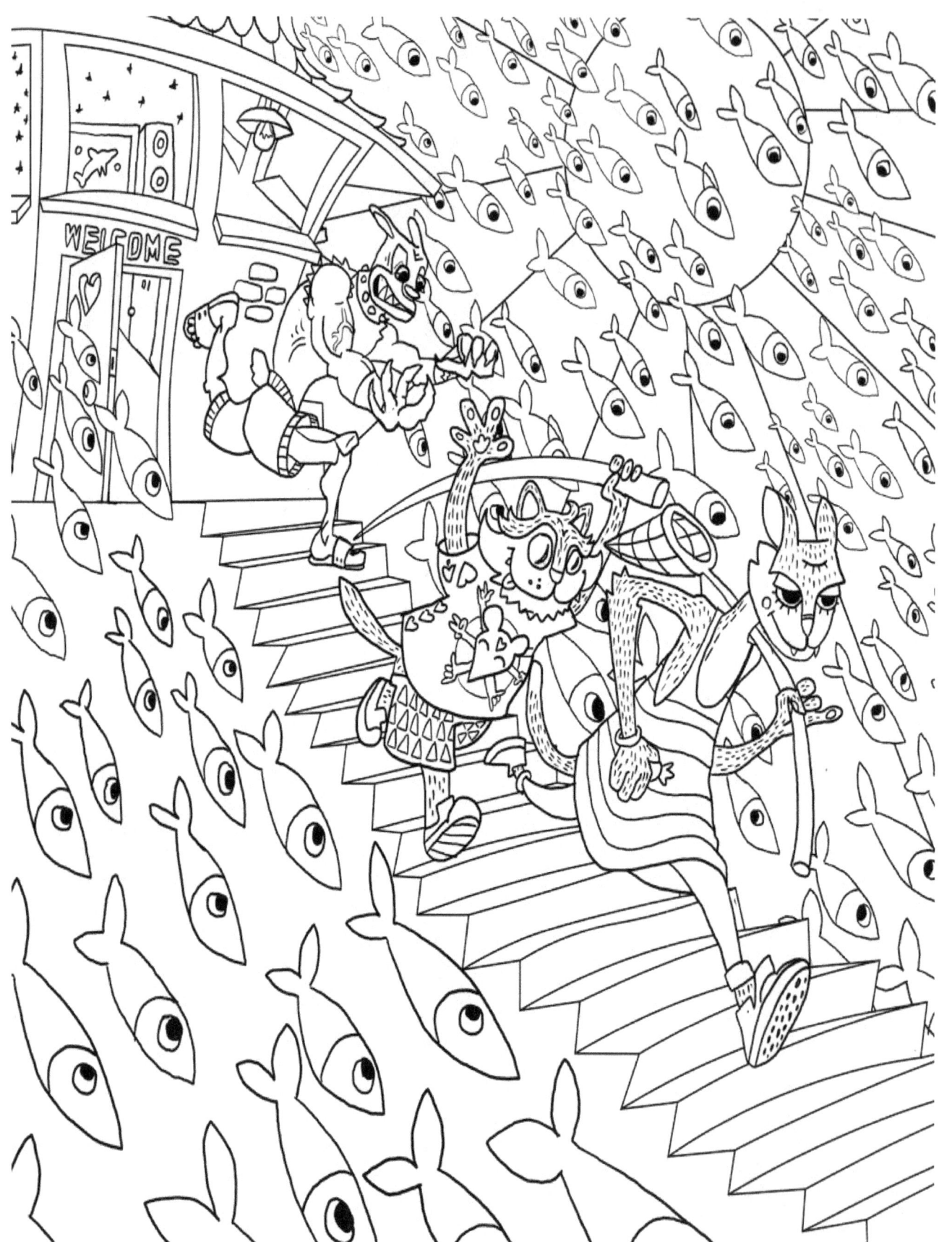

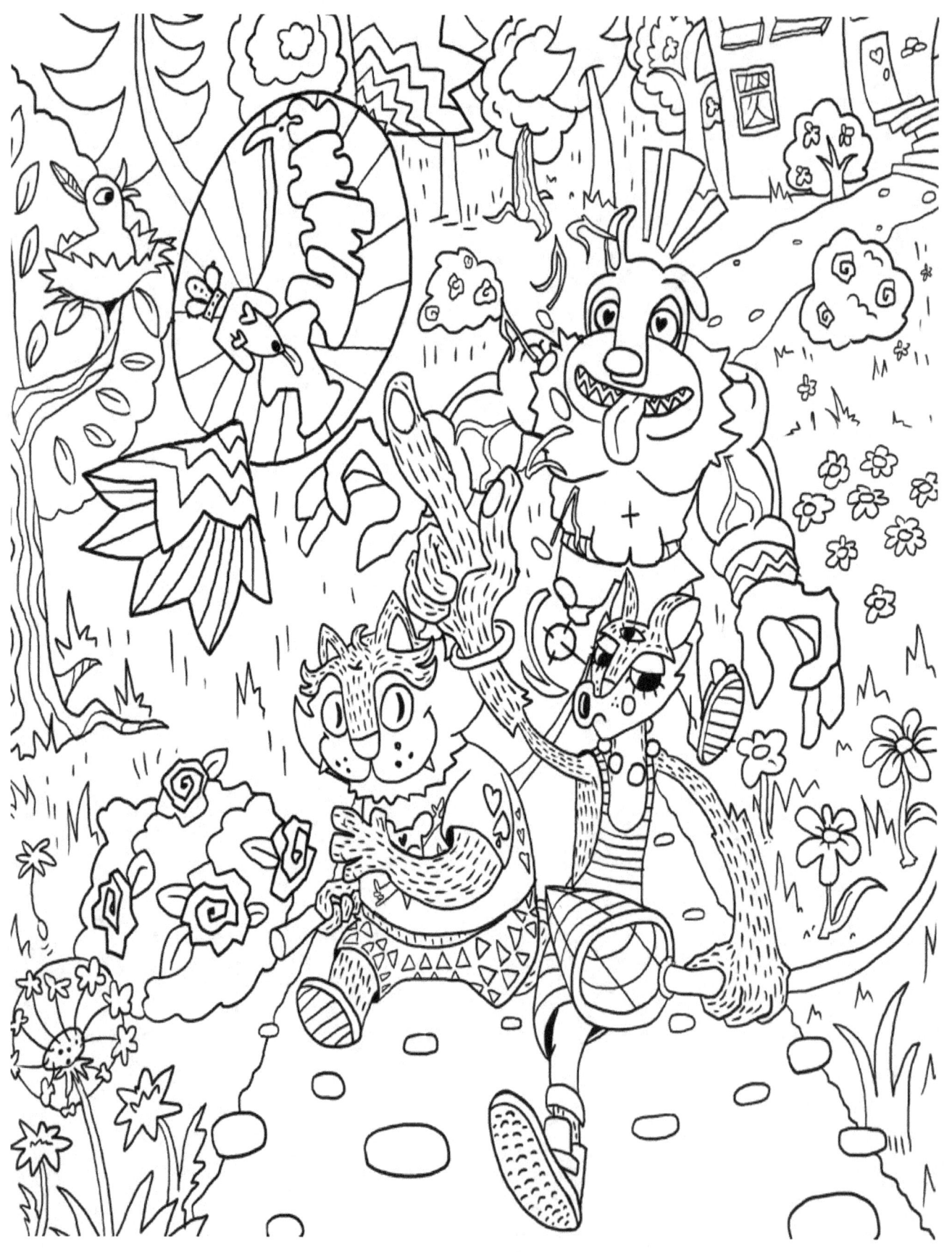

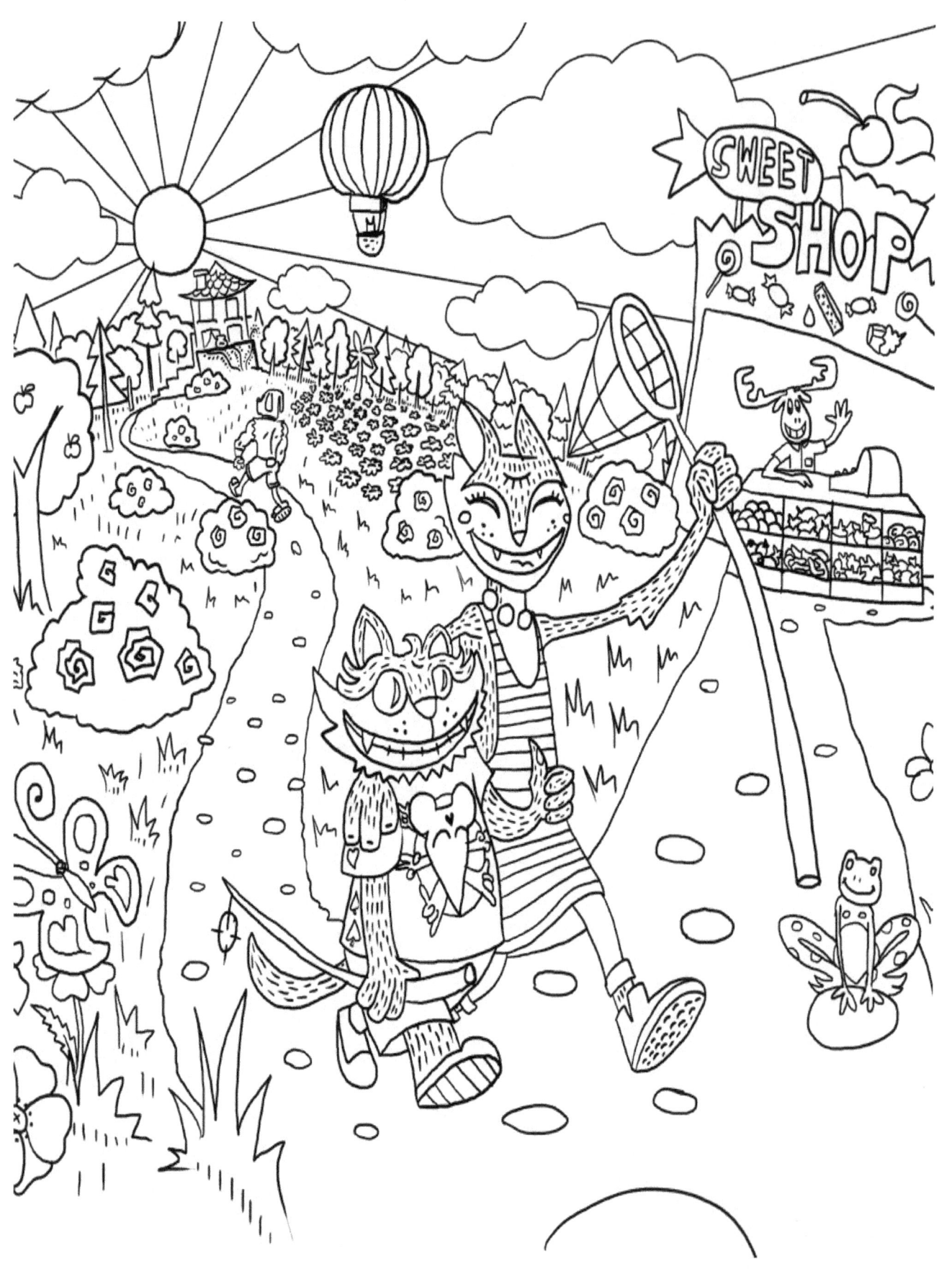

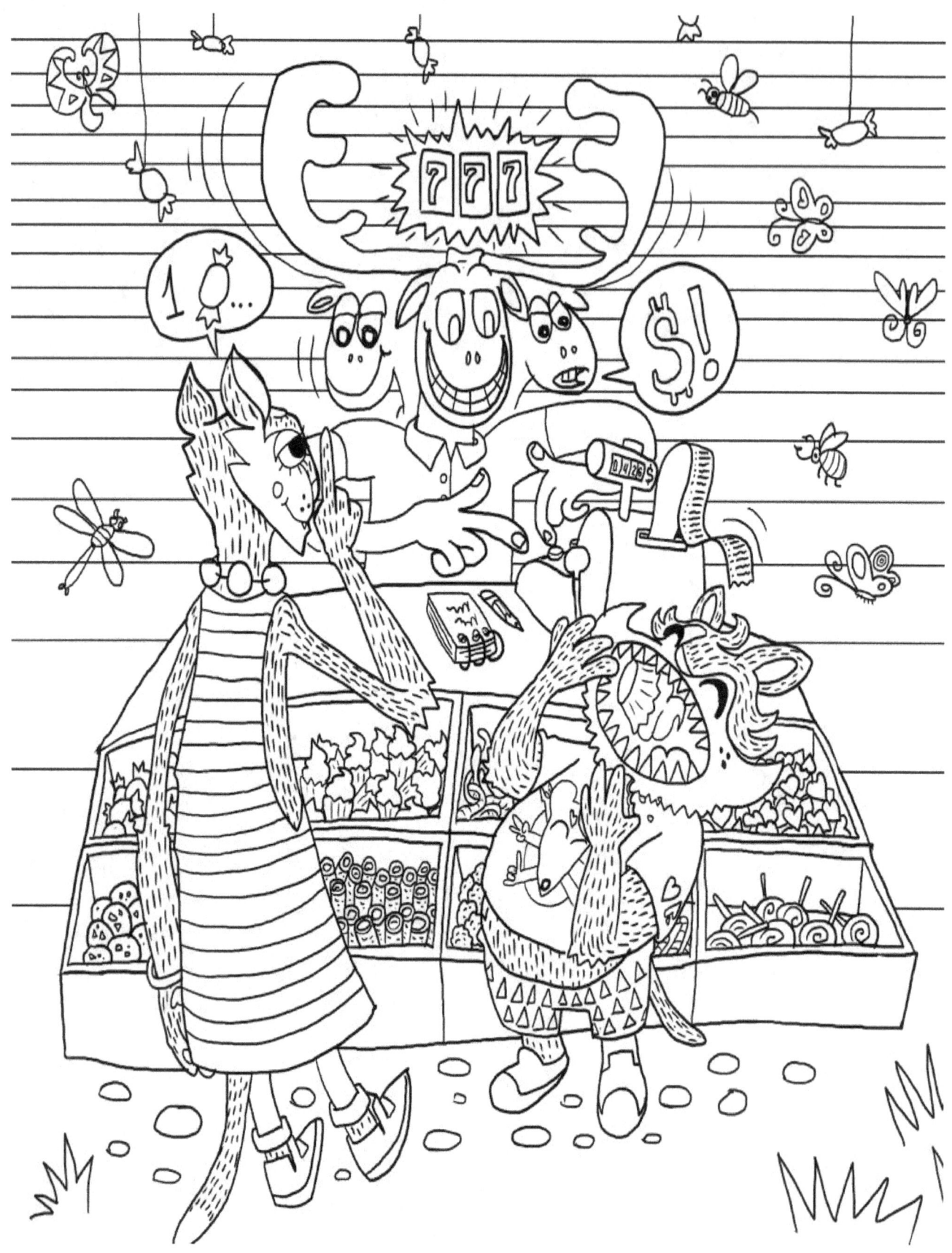

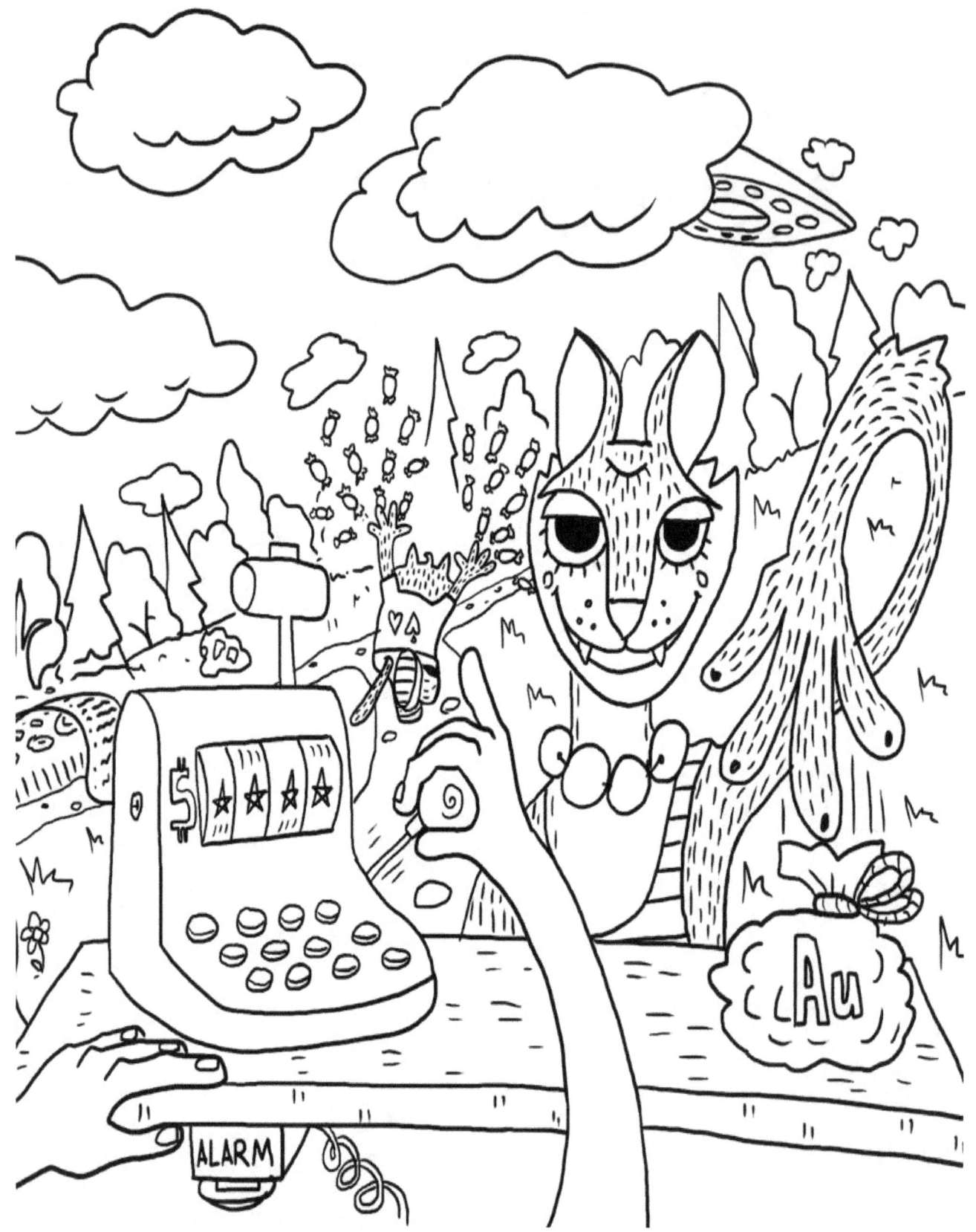

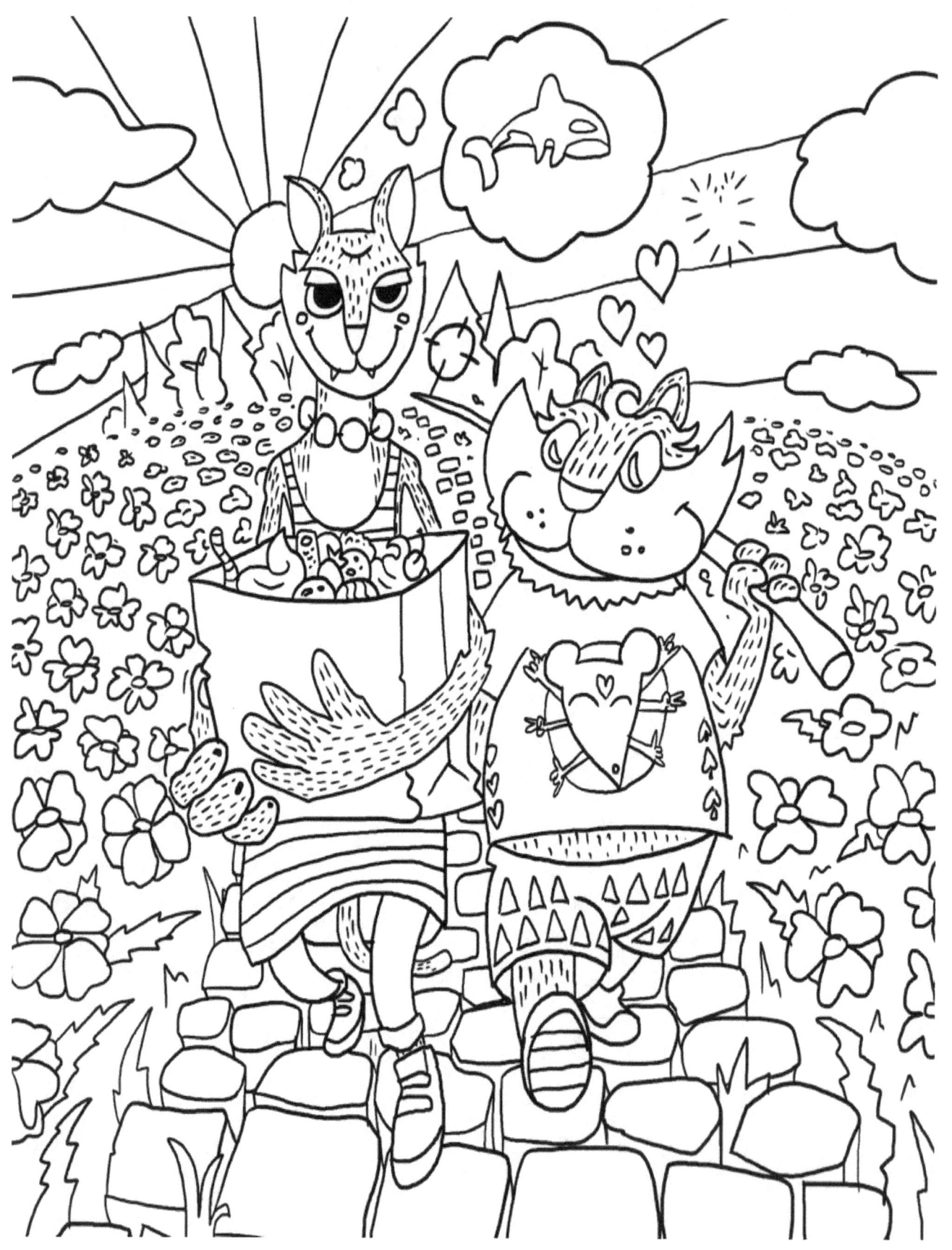

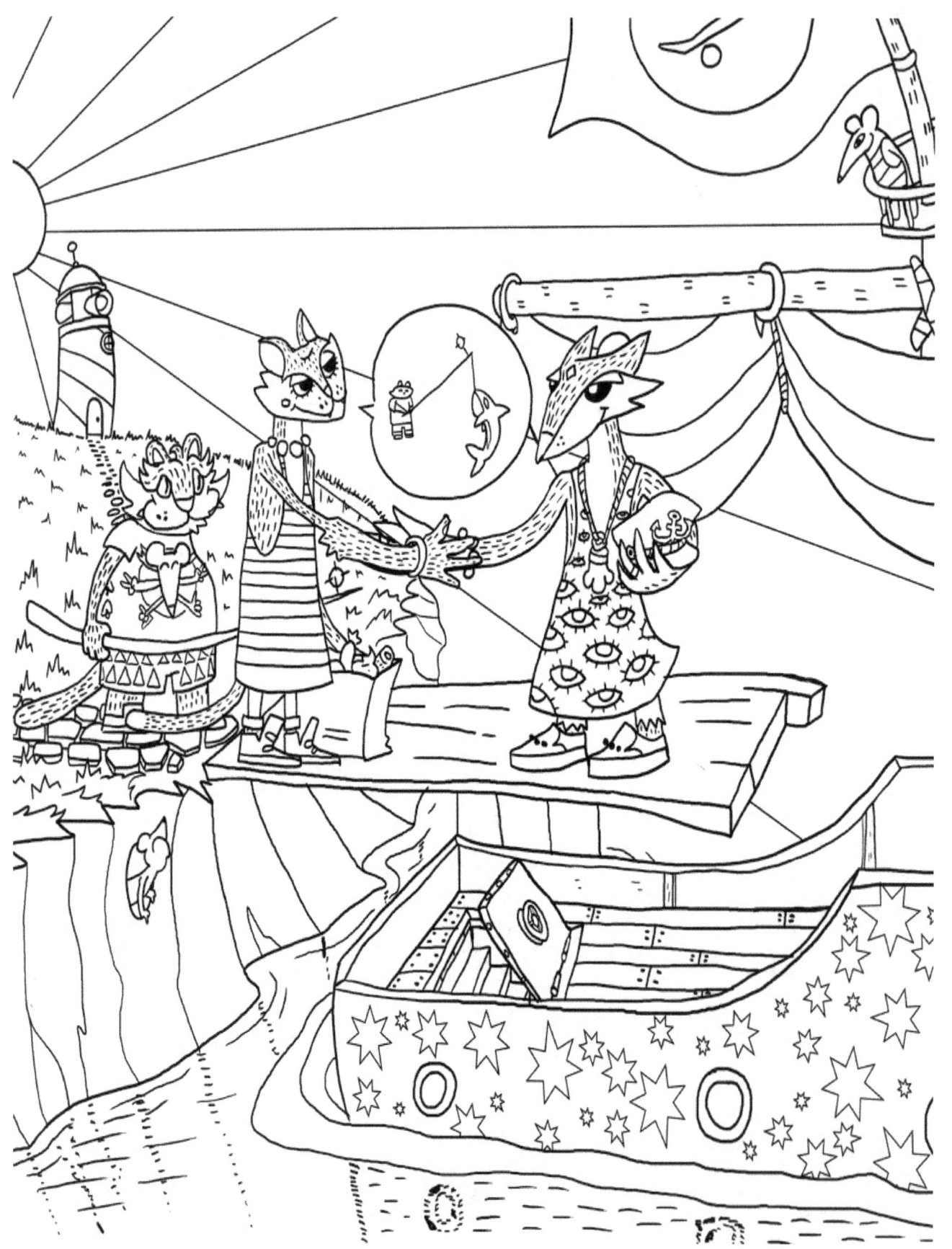

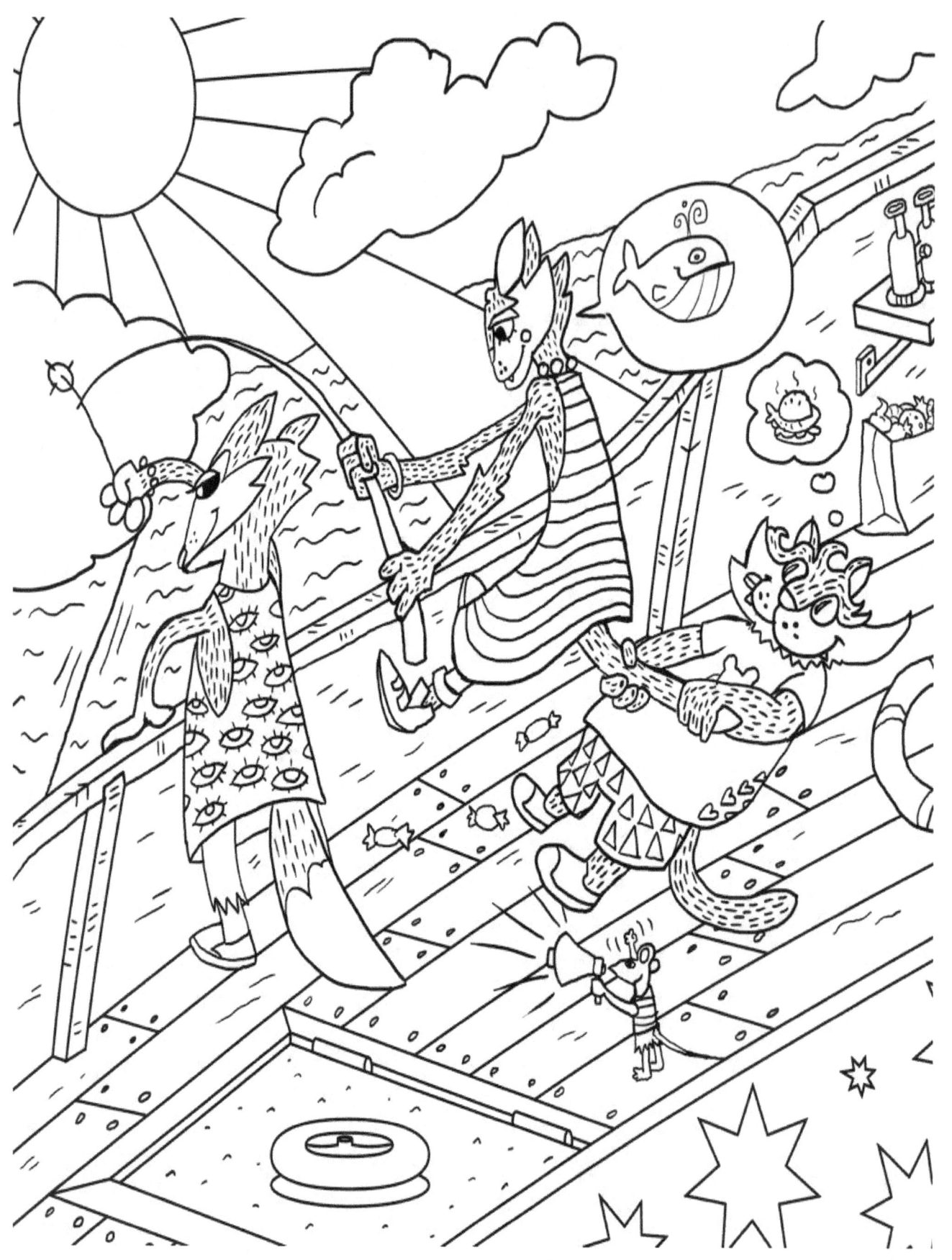

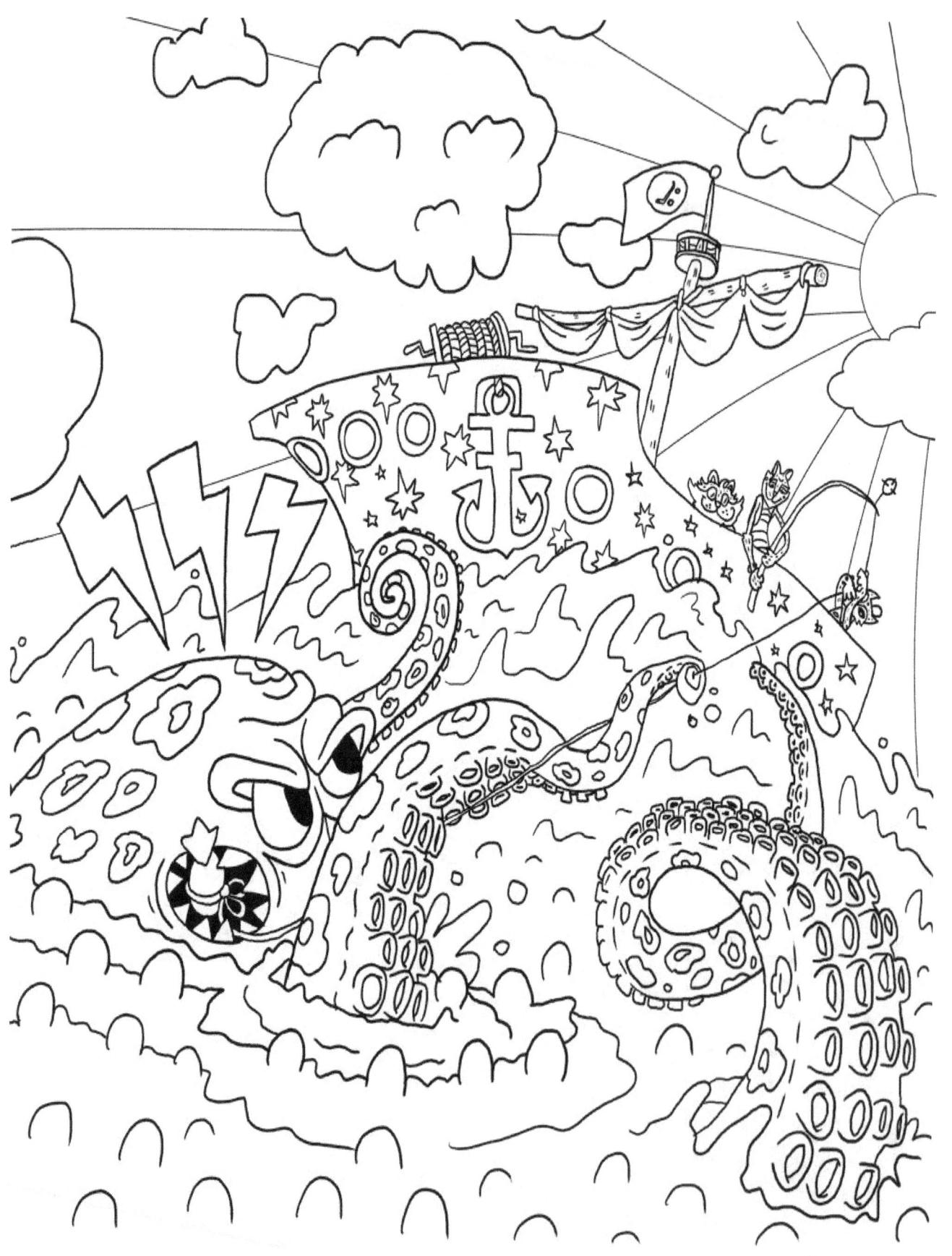

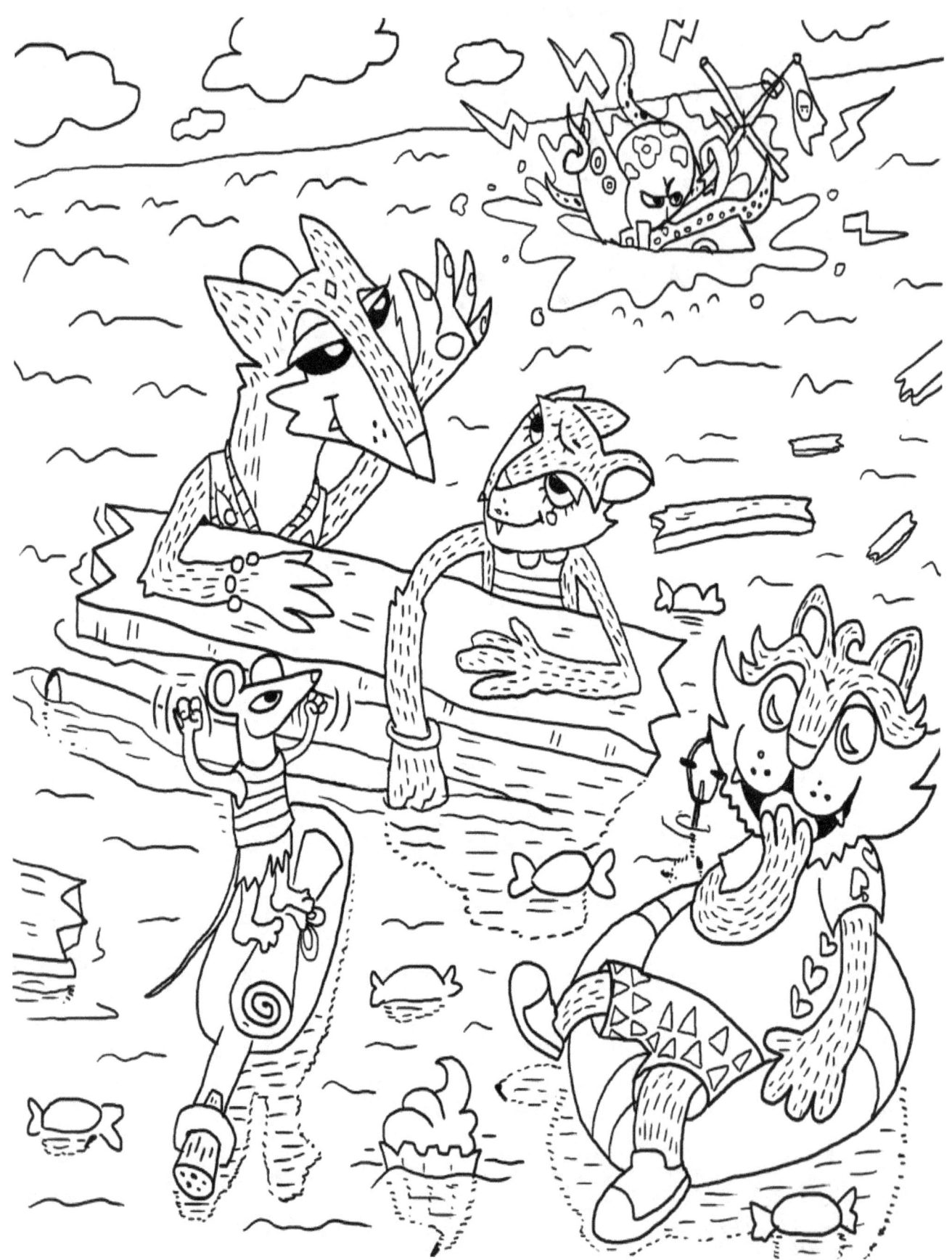

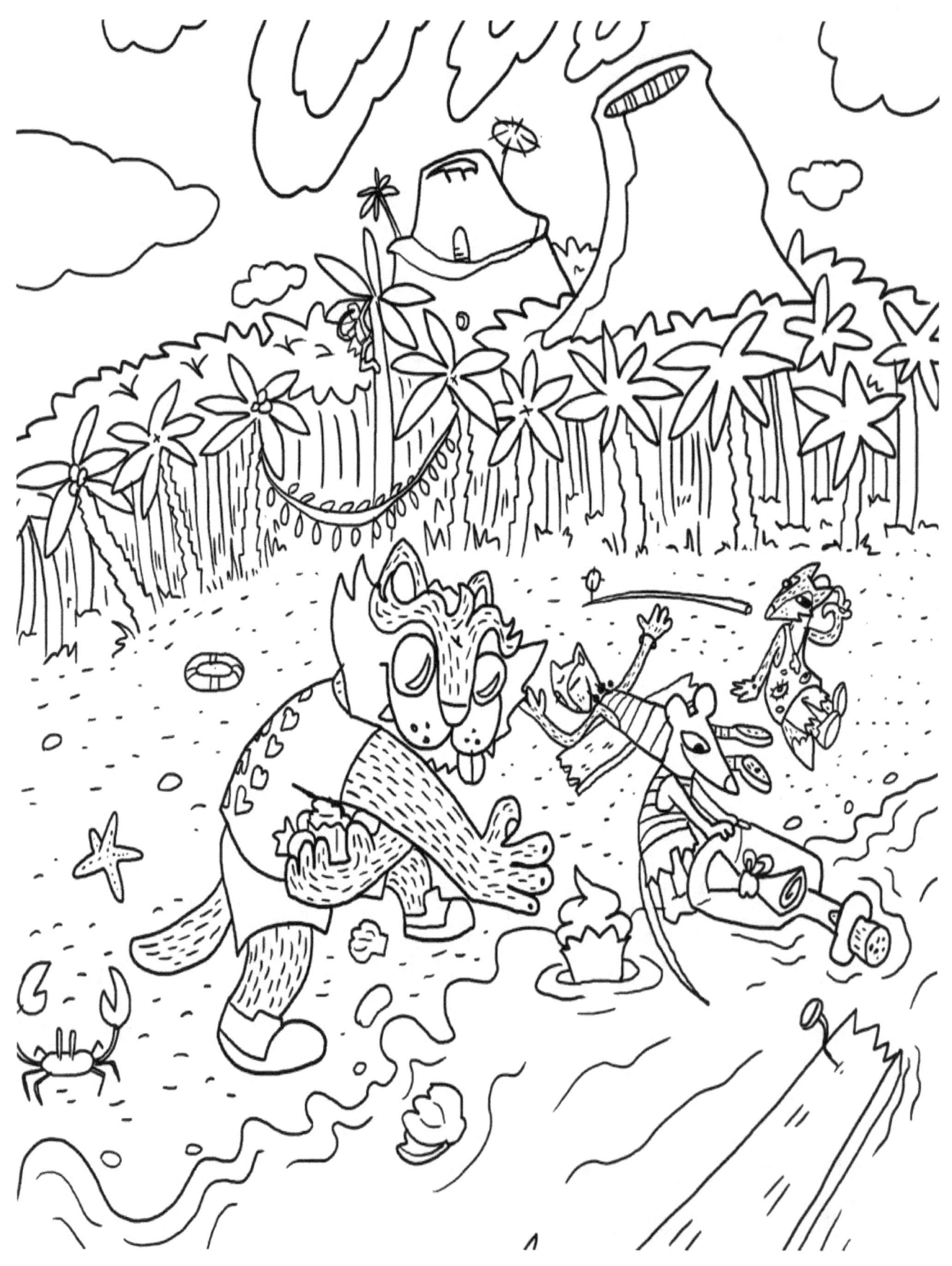

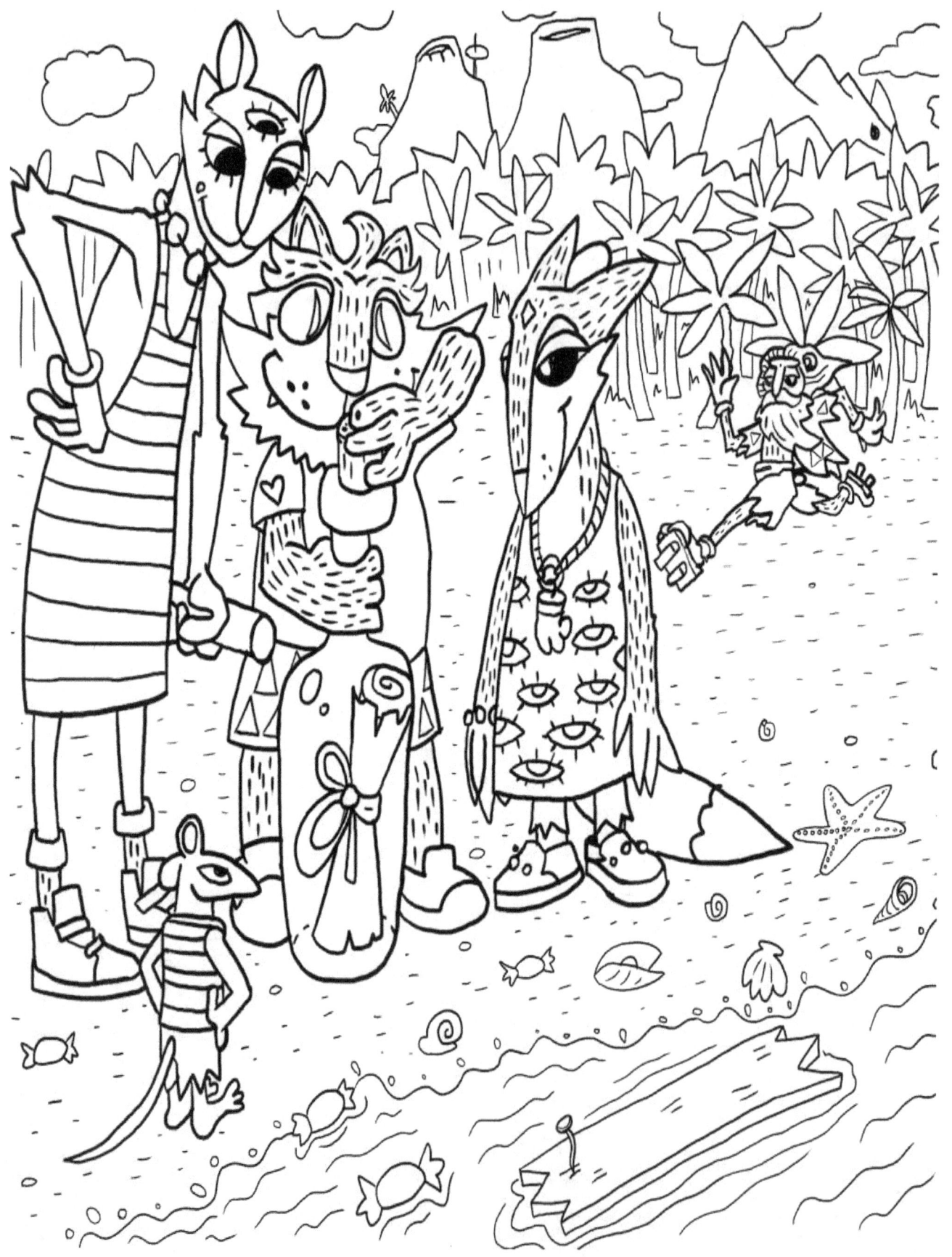

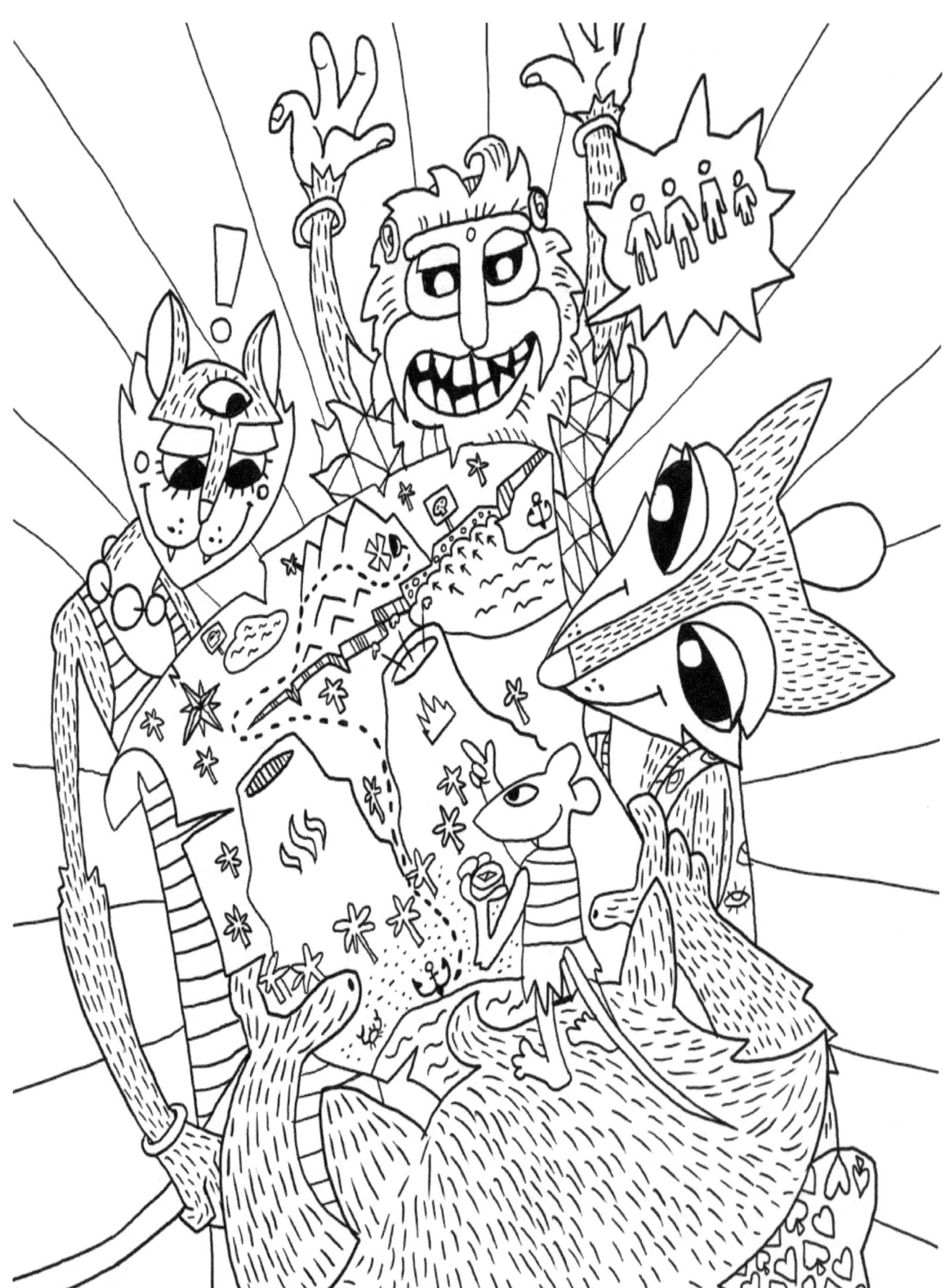

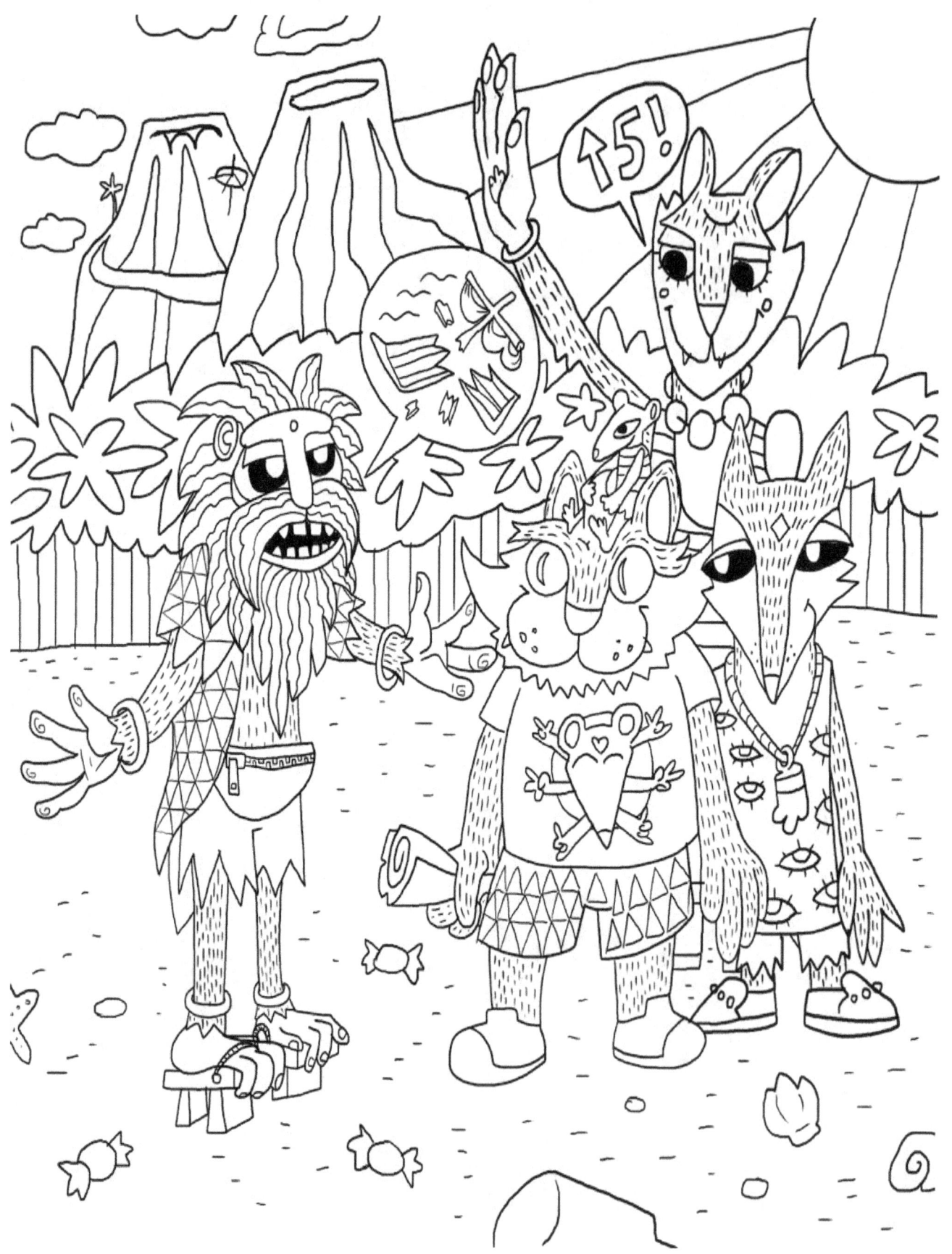

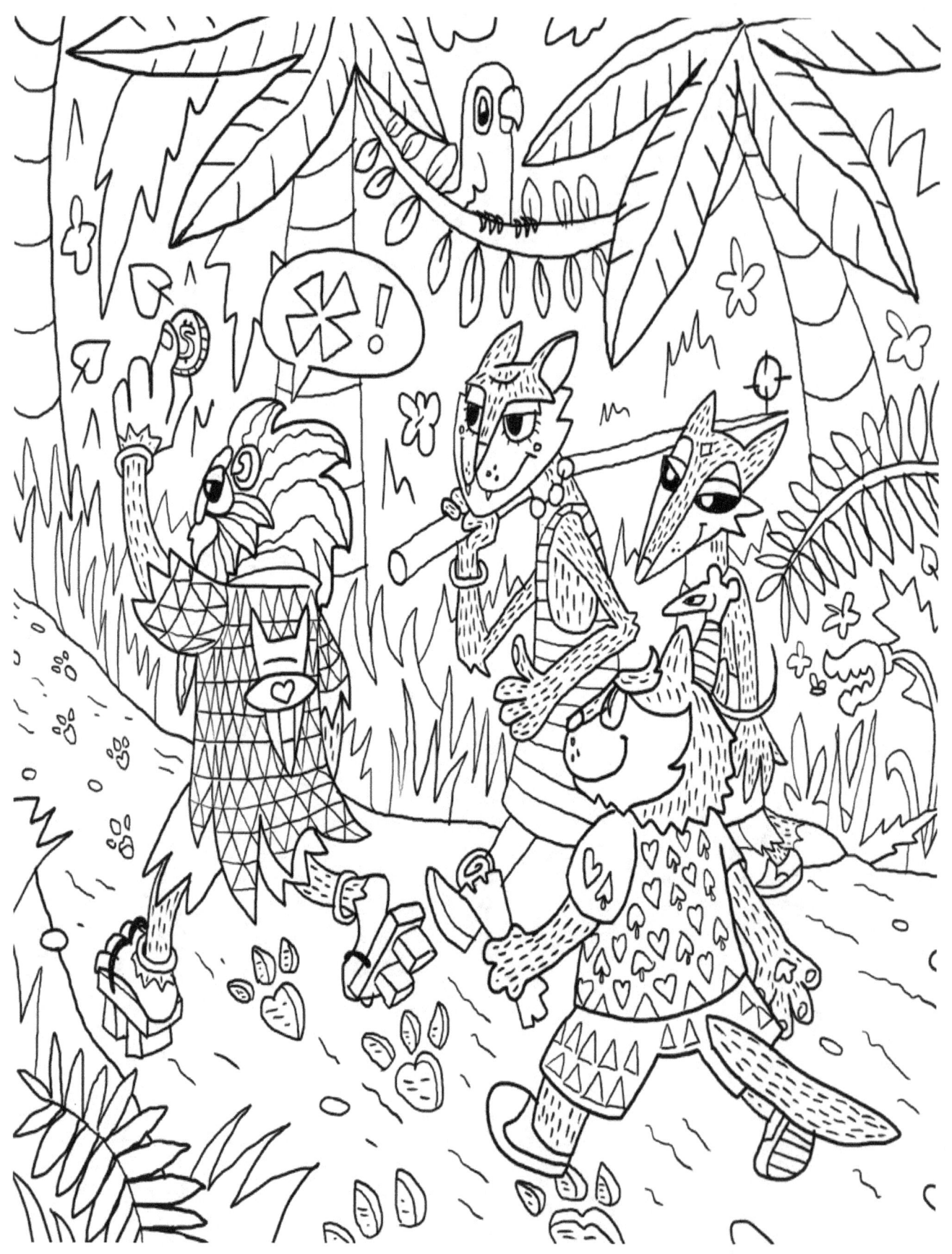

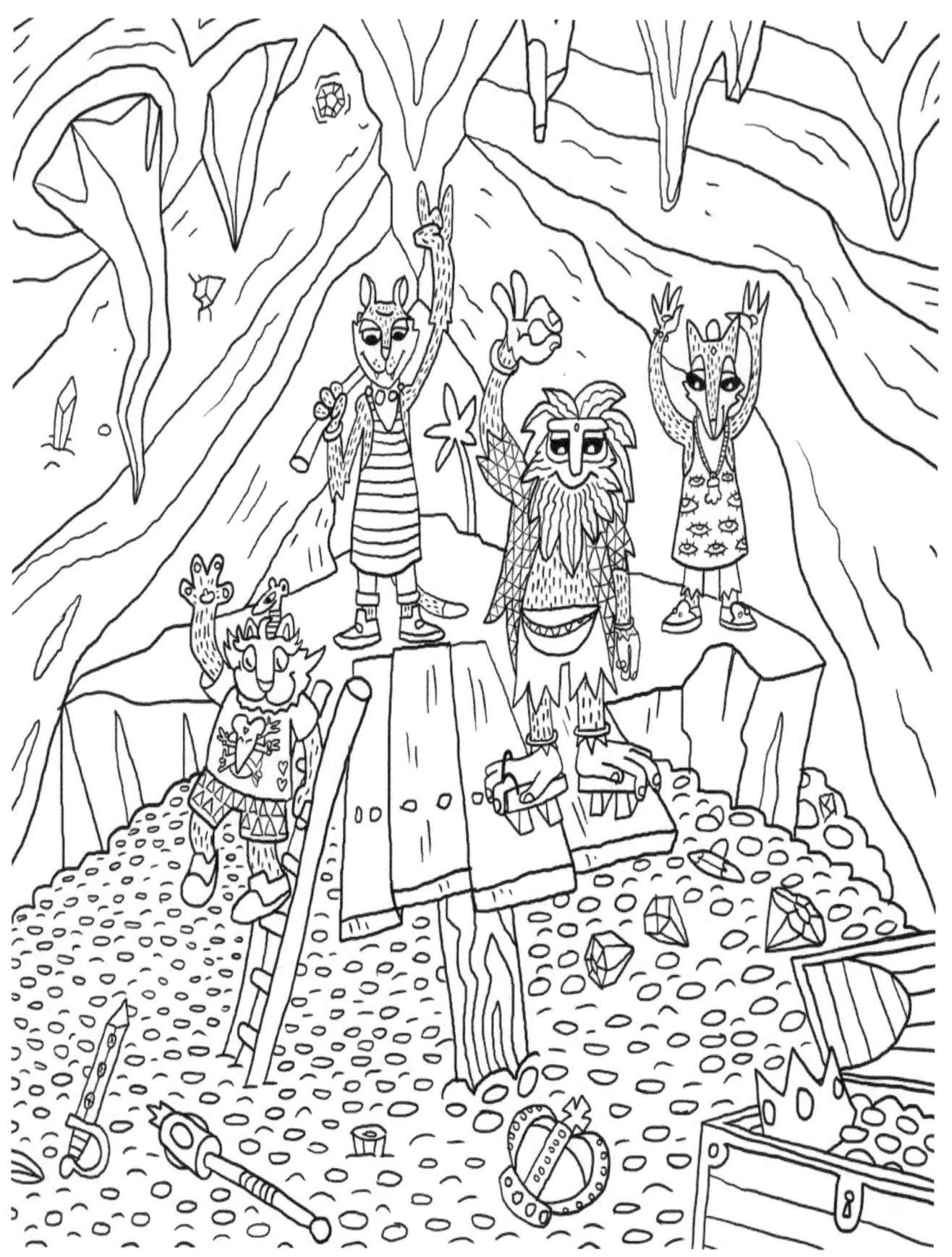

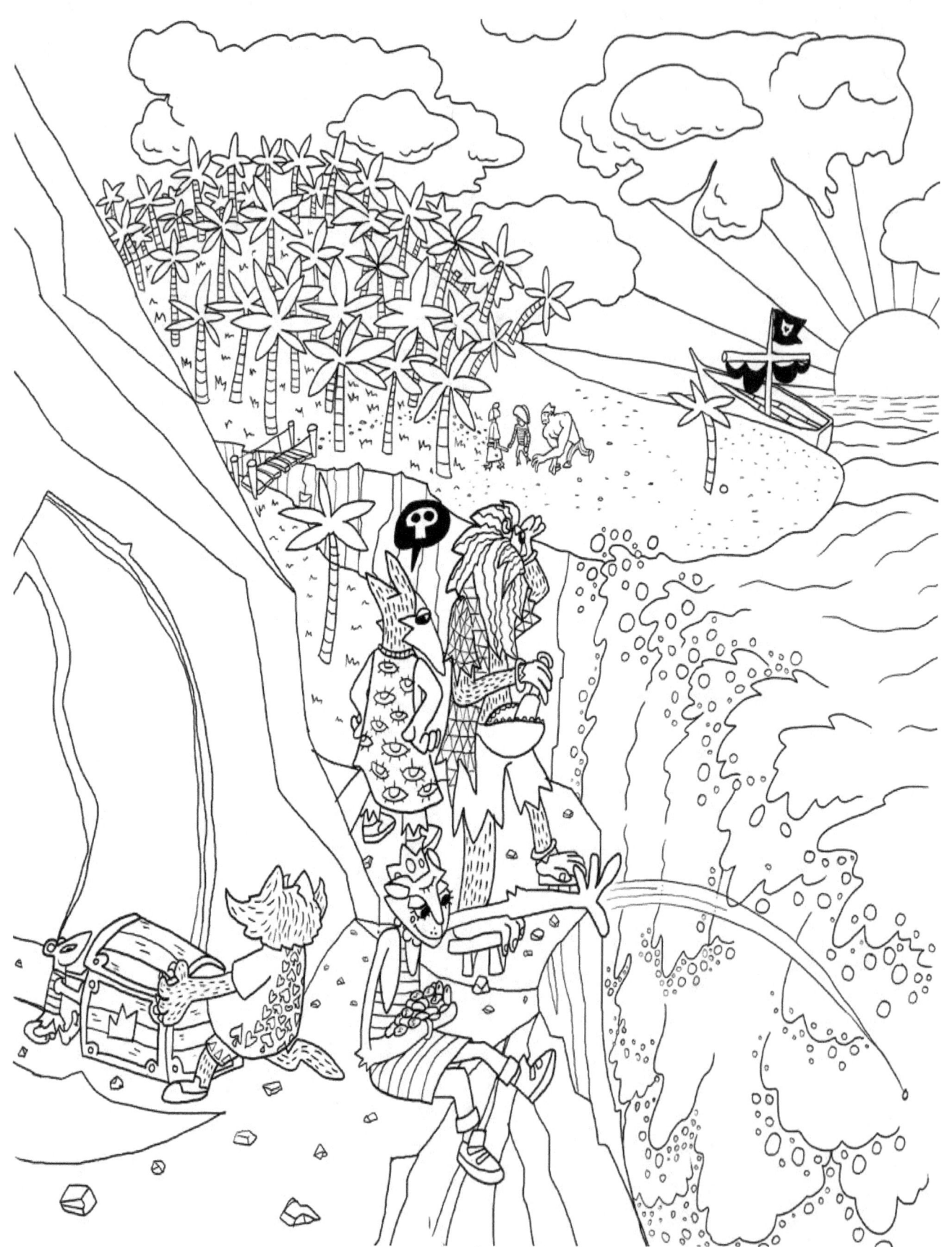

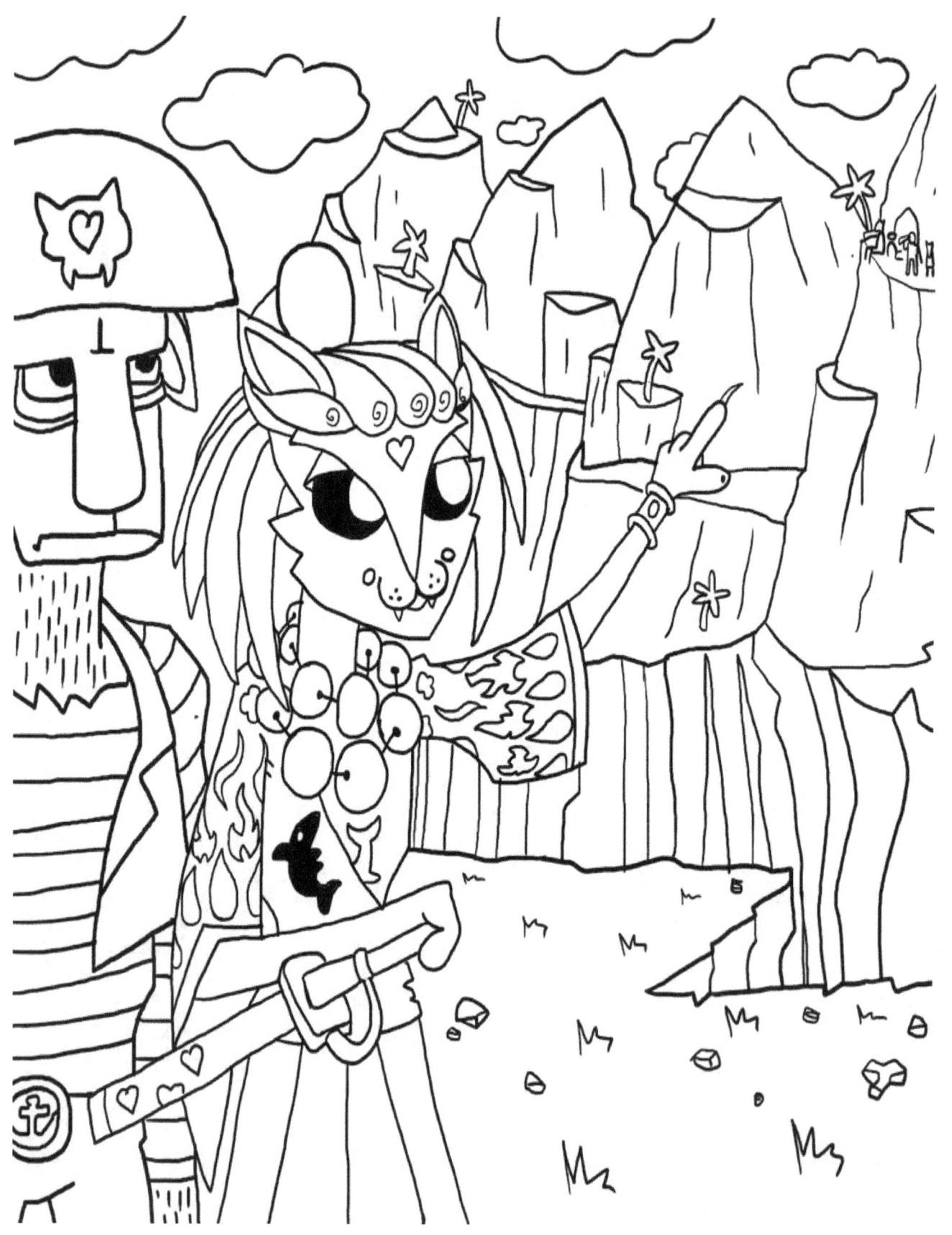

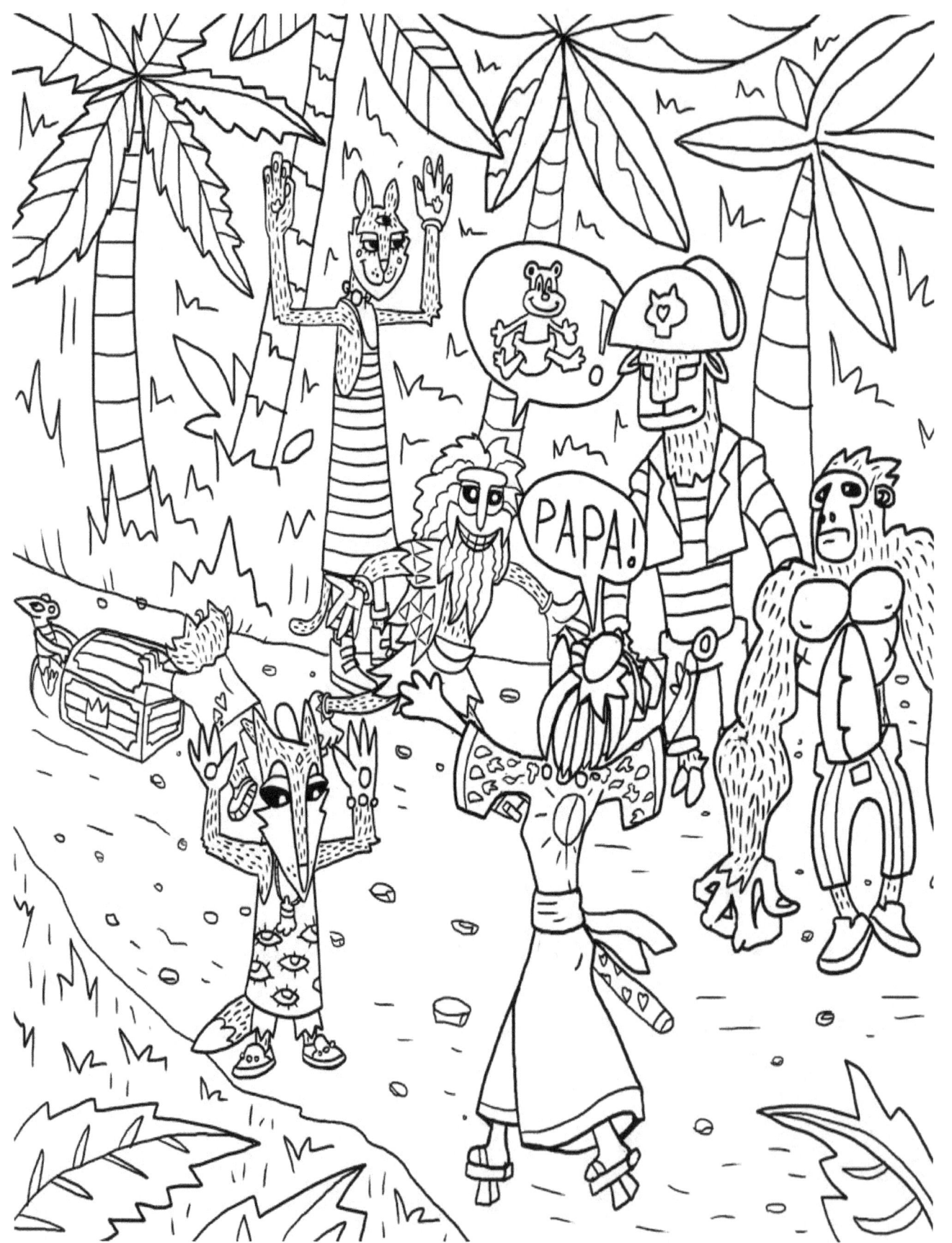

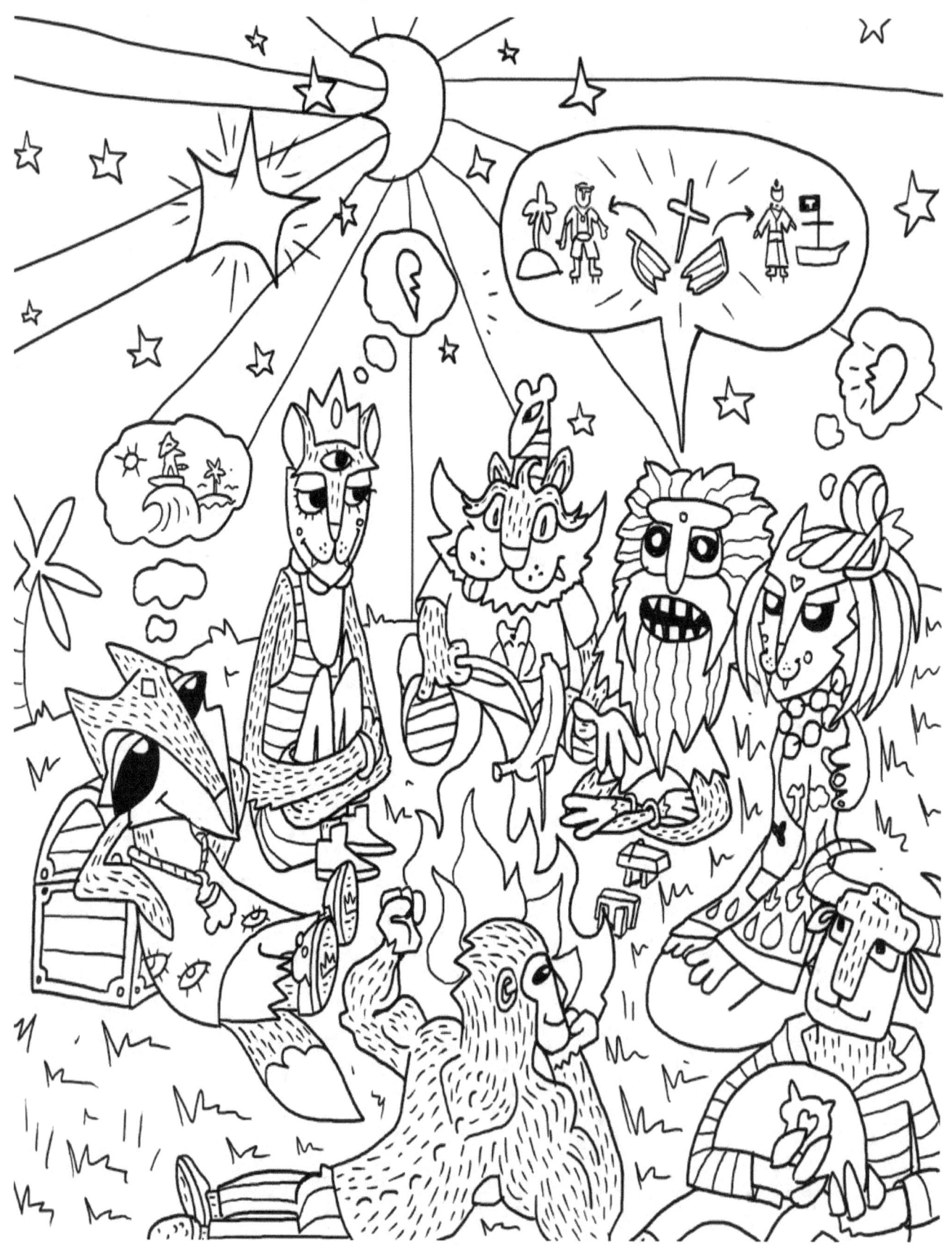

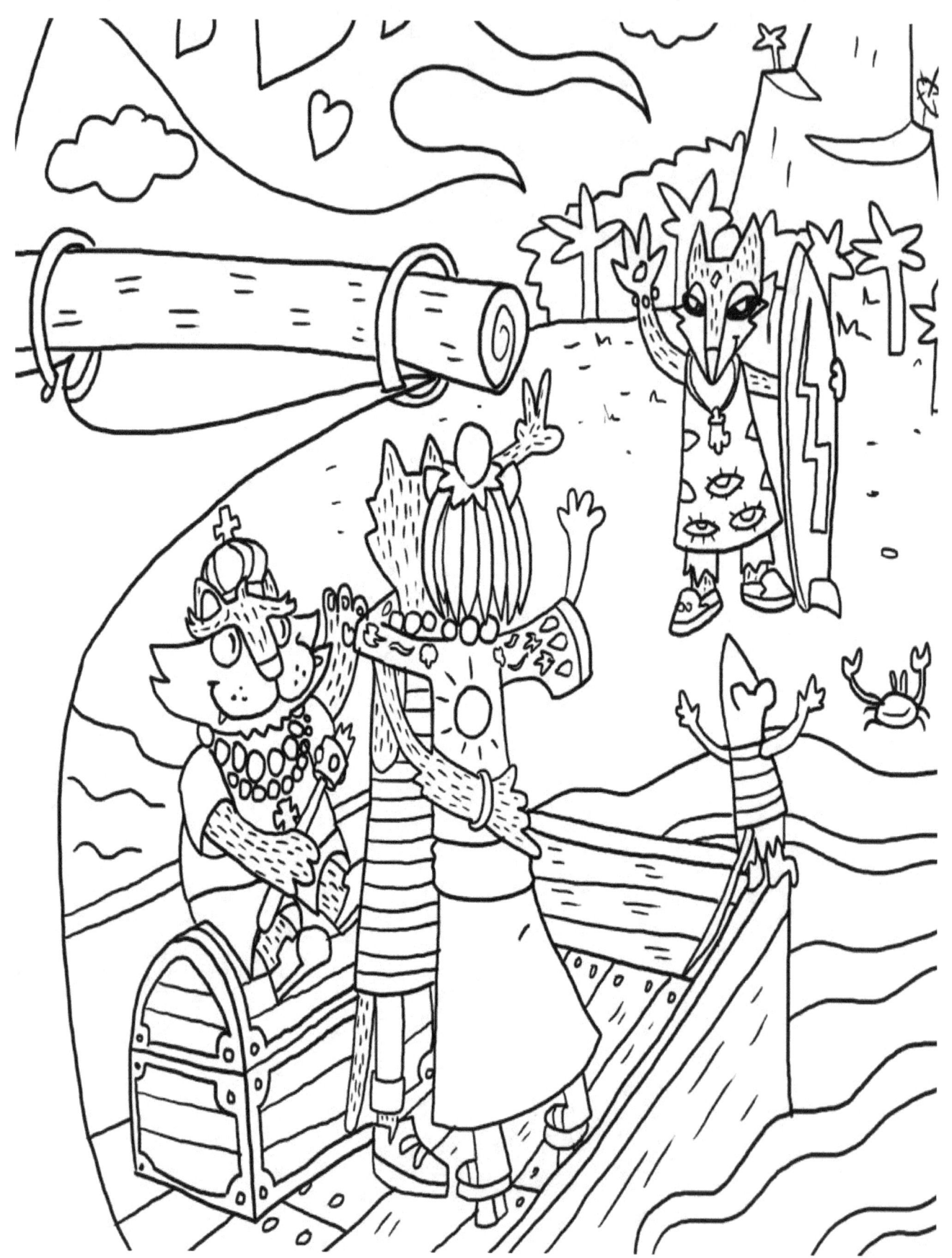

www.ingramcontent.com/pod-product-compliance
Lightning Source LLC
Chambersburg PA
CBHW081226170526
45165CB00009B/2974